DATE DUE

DEMCO 128-5046

The Earth's Layers

Where there is land, the crust is 15 to 35 miles (24–56 km) thick. Under the ocean it is 3 to 5 miles (4.8–8 km) thick.

The mantle is 1,800 miles (2,900 km) thick.

The inner core is 1,600 miles (2,500 km) across.

The outer core is 1,400 miles (2,200 km) thick.

It's hard to imagine, but deep beneath your feet there is hot, melted rock!

When Things Heat Up

For people to take advantage of geothermal energy, heat from deep inside the Earth must rise closer to the surface. So how does this happen?

The Earth's crust is broken into large pieces, called **tectonic plates**, which fit together like a giant jigsaw puzzle. In places where the tectonic plates meet up, there are cracks in the Earth's crust that allow magma from the mantle to come closer to the surface. Most of the time, magma is trapped underground, but sometimes we see it flow or explode from a **volcano**.

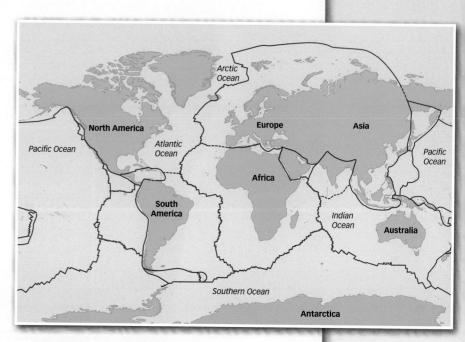

The red lines on this map show the edges of the Earth's tectonic plates.

When water from above ground seeps into cracks in the Earth's crust, that water gathers in underground pools, trapped between rocks. If superhot magma rises into the crust close to a pool, it then heats this water. These underground pools of extremely hot water are called **geothermal reservoirs**, and it is this water that allows us to capture the Earth's internal heat.

In most places it's not possible to see that there is a geothermal reservoir under the ground. Sometimes, however, the hot water escapes onto the surface and creates **geysers** and **hot springs**, or pools.

How a Geothermal Reservoir Forms

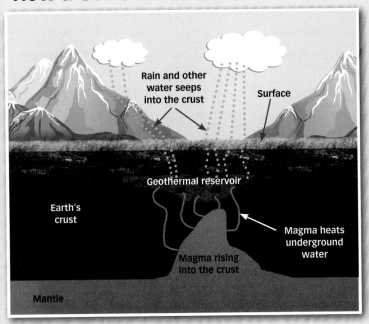

Rain and other water seeps into the crust

Surface

Geothermal reservoir

Earth's crust

Magma rising into the crust

Magma heats underground water

Mantle

Tourists watch as Old Faithful erupts.

Magma

When magma reaches the Earth's surface, it is called lava.

Lava

Hot-Tubbing

Using geothermal energy is not a new idea—people have been doing it for thousands of years! When heated water from a geothermal reservoir formed a hot spring on the Earth's surface, the water could be used for cooking, doing laundry, and bathing.

Around the year AD 60, the Romans built a large bathing complex at a hot spring in the city that is now known as Bath, in southwest England. The spring is fed by geothermal reservoirs that are up to 14,000 feet (4,300 m) underground. Every day, around 240,000 gallons (908,000 l) of hot water bubbles to the surface at this spring. The centerpiece of the Roman baths was a huge bathing pool filled with the naturally heated water. Visitors from all over the **Roman Empire** came to bathe in the pool.

Tourists still visit the Roman baths in Bath today, although it's no longer possible to bathe in the pool. There are hot springs worldwide, however, which people do use as natural hot tubs. Many people believe that the **minerals** in hot springs give the waters healing powers.

FAST FACT

The Roman name for the city of Bath was Aquae Sulis, *which means "the waters of Sulis." The 5-foot-(1.6 m) deep bathing pool at Bath was originally inside a large hall with a ceiling that rose 130 feet (40 m) above the pool.*

In Japan, Japanese macaque monkeys bathe in hot springs in winter to keep warm!

The bathing pool at the Roman baths, in Bath, England

Geothermal Power Today

In our modern world, using a hot spring for everyday bathing and doing the laundry isn't really a practical option. So how can the hot water and heat from geothermal reservoirs be used today?

Hot Water: From the Earth's Crust to Your Home

Naturally heated hot water can be pumped from deep underground. Then it can be delivered through pipes directly to faucets in homes, schools, and other buildings. Warmth from hot water can also be used to heat buildings.

Hot Water and Steam: Making Electricity

Most electricity power stations operate by burning coal inside huge boilers that heat water to such a high temperature that it becomes steam. Then the steam is used to turn giant **turbines** that generate electricity. At geothermal power stations, naturally produced superhot water and steam from underground is used to drive the turbines.

Worldwide, engineers and scientists are working to further develop the ways in which we use geothermal power. But why do we need to do this when we have coal to burn in power stations, and our heat and hot water can be supplied by systems powered by electricity, oil, and **natural gas**?

FAST FACT

Hot water from geothermal sources can be used in many ways to heat buildings. In some systems, hot water flows through pipes into heaters that collect heat from the water and then blow the heat into the air. The cooled water is then piped back to the underground geothermal reservoir to be reheated and reused.

This pipeline from the Nesjavellir geothermal power plant delivers nearly 500 gallons (1,900 l) of naturally-heated hot water to Reykjavik, Iceland, every second.

The Nesjavellir power plant in Iceland is one of several geothermal power plants that produce electricity and hot water for Reykjavik, the country's capital city.

Why Do We Need New Energy?

We need to find new sources of energy because coal, oil, and natural gas, the main fuels we use today, are running out. Also, our use of these fuels is causing a gradual increase in Earth's temperatures which is leading to **climate change**.

Coal, oil, and gas are called **fossil fuels**. They formed deep underground from the remains of animals and plants. These fuels took millions of years to form, but now they are running out, and we cannot make more.

When we burn natural gas, oil, or coal, gases such as carbon dioxide, methane, and nitrous oxide are released into the Earth's **atmosphere**. Known as **greenhouse gases**, these gases trap the Sun's heat on Earth, just as a greenhouse traps heat inside.

We need heat on Earth, but if temperatures rise too much, ocean levels will rise, because water expands when it is heated. Also, ice at the North and South Poles will melt. This could cause low-lying coastal places, such as New York City, to flood. Other places could become so hot and dry that people will be unable to grow crops or find water.

In most people's homes, water for a hot shower is heated by electricity or by a boiler that burns oil or natural gas.

When coal is burned to produce electricity, like here, at the Big Bend power station in Florida, greenhouse gases are released into the atmosphere.

FAST FACT

Oil, natural gas, and coal formed when plants and animals died and their remains settled on the ocean floor and at the bottom of swamps.

300 to 400 million years ago

Ocean

300 to 400 million years ago

Over time, the remains were buried by layers of soil or water.

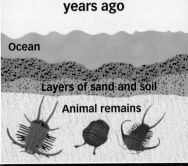

50 to 100 million years ago

Ocean

Layers of sand and soil

Animal remains

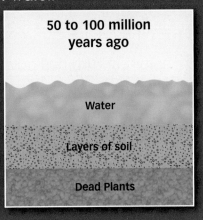

50 to 100 million years ago

Water

Layers of soil

Dead Plants

Heat and pressure turned the remains to oil, natural gas, and coal that we extract from deep underground.

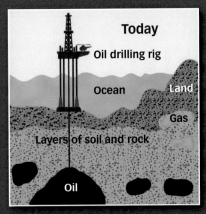

Today

Oil drilling rig

Ocean

Land

Gas

Layers of soil and rock

Oil

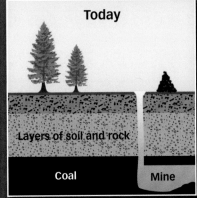

Today

Layers of soil and rock

Coal

Mine

Geothermal Electricity

Using geothermal power is one of the most environmentally-friendly ways to make electricity.

Power stations that use this type of energy have to be built on top of a geothermal reservoir. The reservoir is usually 1 to 2 miles (1.6–3.2 km) below the surface.

Some geothermal reservoirs contain both hot water and steam. Others are so hot that all the water turns to steam. Dry steam geothermal power stations pipe steam from steam-only reservoirs to the surface. Flash steam power stations pipe water that has reached temperatures as high as 700°F (370°C) to the surface. The water is so hot that some becomes steam. In both cases, the steam is then used to turn the power station's turbines at 3,600 revolutions per minute. The spinning turbines power **generators** that produce the electricity.

Geothermal power stations have two main advantages over coal-fired power stations. Because fossil fuels are not being burned, no greenhouse gases are released as the electricity is produced. And unlike coal, which is running out, heat from inside the Earth is a continuous power source that will never run out.

FAST FACT

The United States produces more electricity using geothermal power than any other country in the world. Most US geothermal power stations are in western states and Hawaii because these regions have more geothermal reservoirs than elsewhere in the country. California generates more geothermal electricity than any other state.

A steam-driven turbine used in the production of electricity at a power station

15

The Geysers

The Geysers is a vast complex of geothermal power stations in California. The plant produces electricity in a way that does not harm the environment.

Each year, The Geysers generates enough electricity to power 725,000 homes, or a city the size of San Francisco. It is responsible for 20 percent of the green energy produced in California.

As in all geothermal power stations, the steam used at The Geysers is recycled after it is used. Once the steam has gone through the turbines, it is cooled down. The steam then condenses into water and is piped back into the underground reservoir so it can be naturally reheated and used again.

At The Geysers, this recycling has been taken one step further. Programs have been put in place to recycle wastewater from surrounding communities to increase the amount of water, and therefore steam, available to the power stations. From just one area, Santa Rosa, a 41-mile-(66 km) long pipeline pipes 11 million gallons (42 million l) of wastewater every day from homes and businesses into The Geyser's underground geothermal reservoirs.

To extract steam or water from inside the Earth's crust, large drills carve a well that reaches from the surface to the reservoir below. Then, like a drinking straw reaching deep into the bottom of a soda bottle, a pipe is inserted into the well to draw up the steam or hot water.

This simple diagram shows how steam is extracted from a geothermal reservoir, used in a power station, and then recycled.

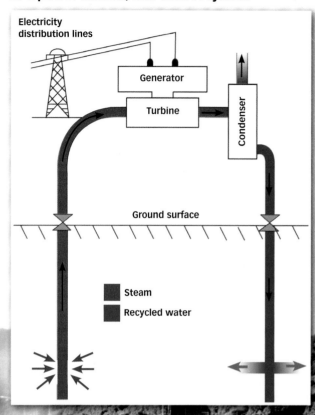

Electricity distribution lines

Generator

Turbine

Condenser

Ground surface

Steam

Recycled water

A geothermal power plant at The Geysers complex in California

A Geothermal Success Story

Iceland is situated where two of Earth's major tectonic plates meet up. This makes for a high level of geothermal activity and has helped Iceland become one of the world's greenest countries.

For many years, Iceland relied on imported oil as a major source of energy. In the 1970s, however, oil prices were rising and supplies from oil-producing countries in the Middle East were threatened due to worldwide political disputes. The Icelandic government decided to develop new types of homegrown energy.

Just a few decades later, 100 percent of Iceland's electricity is supplied via **renewable**, green methods, with 20 percent coming from geothermal power stations.

The Blue Lagoon at the Svartsengi geothermal power station, in Iceland

In Reykjavik, the capital city, 95 percent of buildings are heated by systems that use hot water pumped from geothermal reservoirs. Over 800 miles (1,300 km) of pipes carry hot water directly from underground reservoirs to the city's hot-water faucets.

Today, Reykjavik is one of the most environmentally-friendly cities in the world. It saves up to 4 million tons (3.6 million t) of damaging carbon dioxide from being released into the atmosphere each year.

Iceland—Geothermal Power in Action

Iceland can use its green power to attract some types of business to its shores.

Large companies and organizations have data centers where a computer system holds all the company's data. For example, a bank will have a data center where information about its customers and their accounts is held. Data centers use massive amounts of electricity to power the computers and keep them at a cool temperature so they do not malfunction.

Iceland can offer companies from outside the country a place to store their data. Iceland's green electricity is cheaper than electricity produced in traditional ways, which will save companies money. Also, for companies that want to lower their carbon footprint—the amount of carbon dioxide produced by the company's activities—storing their data using green electricity will help them achieve this goal.

Data centers consume 1.3 percent of the electricity used worldwide. Iceland can use the environmentally-friendly electricity it produces to make data storage greener, which can help stop climate change.

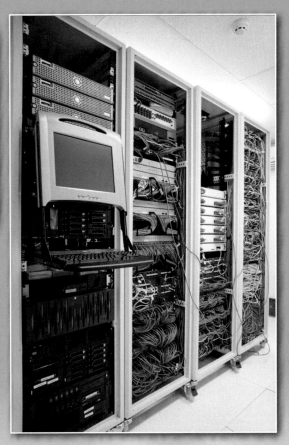

Using geothermal and other green energy sources to power data centers will reduce the amount of greenhouse gases in the atmosphere.

Steam rising from a hot spring is the only clue to the natural power source that is hidden deep below these hills in Iceland.

Hot-Tubbing for Fish and Alligators!

Geothermal power is being used in farming and other industries worldwide.

Farms that raise fish for food, or tropical fish as pets, are warming their ponds and lakes with water heated by geothermal power. Many types of fish need water at a warm temperature in order to grow and stay healthy. In the past, this water would have been heated using energy from fossil fuels. Now, fish farmers can use naturally heated water from underground to warm up their ponds to the correct temperature.

In Arizona and California, fish farms use geothermal power to raise catfish, bass, and tilapia. Worldwide, fish, eels, giant shrimp, and even alligators are raised using geothermal water.

Some farms use water from underground that is not hot enough to be used in geothermal power stations, but that is hot enough to warm ponds and lakes. At other farms, water that has cooled slightly after being used in a power station, or to heat homes, gets recycled and is used to warm fishponds.

These tasty tomatoes for use in salads or pasta sauces are not sun-dried, but geothermally dried!

FAST FACT

Dried fruits and vegetables are sometimes dried naturally in the Sun. Often, however, they are dried in factories. The heat to dry out these foods can be supplied by systems that run on hot water pumped from geothermal reservoirs.

These alligators are basking in warm water on an alligator farm. The animals are raised for their meat and skins.

The Heat Beneath Your Home!

Most of us don't live in places where there are geothermal reservoirs under the ground. We can, however, still take advantage of Earth's natural heat.

In summer, it might be very hot where you live. In winter, it may be very cold. About 10 feet (3 m) below the ground, however, the temperature is always 50° to 60°F (10°–16°C). This constant underground warmth can be used to heat buildings instead of using electricity or burning fossil fuels in boilers.

In winter, a geothermal heat pump collects heat from underground and delivers it into a house, school, or office building. In summer, the same pump can collect heat from the building and transfer it into the ground. This cools the building and saves the electricity that would have been used to run an air conditioning system.

Geothermal heat pumps can be expensive, but they are able to use the natural heat that is just below the ground anywhere in the world!

Just 10 feet (3 m) under the ground, there is a renewable source of energy that can heat and cool all these different homes 365 days a year!

FAST FACT

A geothermal heat pump has loops of piping under the ground outside the building. Inside the piping, liquid absorbs heat from the ground. The heated liquid then enters a pump that takes the heat and blows it into the air in the building. In summer, the process is reversed. Heat is sucked from the air by the pump and piped back into the ground.

he Perfect Fuel?

rder to combat climate change, we must lower the amounts of enhouse gases that surround our world. Using geothermal power to urally heat water and buildings or to produce electricity significantly uces the amount of greenhouse gases that enter the atmosphere.

pping climate change is just one of the many benefits that geothermal power rs us. So what are the others? And are there any downsides to using this e of energy?

Geothermal Power Pros

✓ Large amounts of energy are used to transport coal, oil, and gas from where they are extracted from the ground. Geothermal energy is usually produced very close to where it is needed.

✓ Many nations have to buy oil or coal from other countries to supply their power needs. Every country in the world, however, has underground heat that can run geothermal heat pumps. Many also have geothermal reservoirs that can be used to produce electricity, heat, and hot water.

✓ Unlike solar or wind power, geothermal power does not rely on particular types of weather. It can also be produced day or night, 365 days a year.

✓ There will always be geothermal energy inside our planet because heat is continuously produced inside the Earth.

✓ When fossil fuels are burned, acid gases are produced that mix with clouds to produce acid rain. This rain can pollute rivers and lakes, killing animals and plants. Acid rain damages the leaves of plants, adds poisons to the soil that plants take in, and destroys nutrients in the soil that plants need for health and growth. Geothermal power stations release just 3 percent of the acid gases that are produced by power stations that burn fossil fuels.

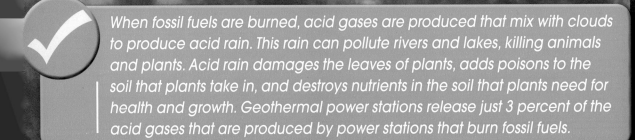

The western United States has more underground "hotspots" than anywhere else in the country.

Geothermal Power Cons

 While there will always be geothermal energy inside the Earth, in some places geothermal reservoirs may cool down over time.

 Setting up a well to extract geothermal power from underground is very expensive. It can cost up to $4 million to drill a well.

 There is a huge amount of geothermal energy inside our planet that could be used to make electricity, but it's not easy to access it. Most places do not have geothermal reservoirs close to the surface.

 Every home could be heated and cooled by a geothermal heat pump, but they are expensive to set up. To buy and install the system can cost up to $30,000.

 While geothermal heat pumps use underground heat to warm the building, the pump itself still needs to be run on electricity. If this electricity has not been produced in an environmentally-friendly way, the system will still be contributing greenhouse gases to the atmosphere.

Powering the Future

The United States is the leading producer of geothermal electricity in the world. In 2011, however, only 0.4 percent of the nation's electricity was generated using geothermal energy. There is still a long way to go!

For decades, explorers, scientists, and engineers have been eager to discover what's in the ocean's depths or beyond our planet in space. Digging deep into the Earth through miles of rock has created less excitement. It could, however, hold the answer to how we both power and save our planet for generations to come.

Geothermal reservoirs are only found close to the surface in a limited number of places on Earth. There is magma below the Earth's crust everywhere on the planet, however. Finding ways to drill deeper and exploit this heat could make geothermal power available to more people.

Our amazing planet gave us oil, natural gas, and coal, but we have almost exhausted the Earth's supplies of these fuels. Now, it's time to fuel our world in a new way by harnessing the power of the heat beneath our feet!

The energy to power our modern world has been deep inside our planet since it formed 4.5 billion years ago.

FAST FACT

Far deeper underground, and in many more places than where hot water geothermal reservoirs form, are areas of rock that have been heated by magma. Scientists, engineers, energy companies, and governments are researching and developing ways to capture the heat from these hot rock reservoirs.

Glossary

atmosphere (AT-muh-sfeer)
The layer of gases surrounding a planet, moon, or star.

climate change (KLY-mut CHAYNJ)
The gradual change in temperatures on Earth. For example, the current warming of temperatures caused by a buildup of greenhouse gases in the atmosphere.

core (KOR)
The mass of solid metal and its outer layer of molten metal at the very center of the Earth.

crust (KRUST)
The outer layer of Earth that is made of rock.

fossil fuels (FO-sul FYOOLZ)
Fuels that formed over millions of years from the remains of plants and animals. Oil, natural gas, and coal are all fossil fuels.

generator (JEH-neh-ray-tur)
A machine that turns mechanical energy, for example the spinning of a turbine, into electrical energy.

geothermal energy
(JEE-oh-ther-mul EN-ur-jee)
Energy in the form of heat inside the Earth

geothermal reservoir
(JEE-oh-ther-mul REH-zuh-vwar)
Water contained in rocks that is heated, usually to a very high temperature, by magma.

geyser (GY-zer)
A place where superheated underground water becomes pressurized in a narrow, rocky passageway in the Earth's crust, and is eventually forced to burst onto the surface.

greenhouse gases
(GREEN-hows GAS-ez)
Gases such as carbon dioxide, methane, and nitrous oxide that occur naturally and are also released into Earth's atmosphere when fossil fuels are burned.

hot spring (HOT SPRING)
A place where hot underground water escapes onto the Earth's surface and forms a pool.

magma (MAG-muh)
Underground rock that has become so hot it melts.

mantle (MAN-tel)
The Earth's middle layer that is partly soild and partly magma.

mineral (MIN-rul)
A naturally occurring solid substance, such as salt or quartz. All rocks contain minerals.

molten (MOHL-ten)
Melted, or liquefied, by heat.

natural gas (NA-chuh-rul GAS)
A fossil fuel that formed underground over millions of years. It is piped to homes and businesses to be used as a source of energy.

renewable (ree-NOO-uh-bul)
A resource that can be produced again and again and will not run out.

Roman Empire (ROH-mun EM-py-ur)
The parts of Europe, Asia, and North Africa that were invaded and then controlled by the Romans.

tectonic plate (tek-TAH-nik PLAYT)
A giant jigsaw-like piece of the Earth's crust.

turbine (TER-byn)
A machine with a wheel or rotor that turns and generates power. A turbine can be driven by gas, water, or steam.

volcano (vol-KAY-noh)
An opening in the surface of Earth that sometimes shoots up a hot liquid rock called lava.

WEBSITES

Due to the changing nature of Internet links, PowerKids Press has developed an online list of websites related to the subject of this book. This site is updated regularly. Please use this link to access the list:

www.powerkidslinks.com/pytt/geo/

Read More

Gleason, Carrie. *Geothermal Energy: Using Earth's Furnace.* Energy Revolution. New York: Crabtree Publishing, 2008.

Hansen, Amy S. *Geothermal Energy: Hot Stuff!.* Powering Our World. New York: PowerKids Press, 2010.

Saunders, Nigel. *Geothermal Energy.* Energy for the Future and Global Warming. New York: Gareth Stevens, 2008.

Index